THE OFFICIAL NEWCASTLE UNITED ANNUAL 2018

Written by Mark Hannen
Designed by Uta Dohlenburg

**Thanks to Michael Bolam, Stan Gate,
Paul Joannou, Rory Mitchinson, and Isobel Reid**

A Grange Publication

© 2017. Published by Grange Communications Ltd., Edinburgh, under licence from Newcastle United Football Club. Printed in the EU.

Photographs © Serena Taylor and Getty Images

ISBN: 978-1-911287-77-3

Welcome to the Official 2018 Newcastle United annual. The Magpies enjoyed a terrific 2016/17 season, winning the Championship under the guidance of Rafa Benítez.

Now, everyone at the club is aiming for a successful 2017/18 season back in the Premier League. Thank you for your continued support and enjoy the read.

Contents

MISSION ACCOMPLISHED
— UNITED ARE THE CHAMPIONS —

The Geordie faithful were in a hugely optimistic mood as the new season approached, and that despite relegation the previous May. Manager Rafa Benítez had remained in the United hot seat after being appointed in March 2016 and after making a number of key signings to replace the likes of Andros Townsend, Gini Wijnaldum and Moussa Sissoko who had left or were leaving Tyneside, the bookies understandably made the Magpies the pre-season favourites to win the Sky Bet Championship. But, after losing the first two games, things weren't exactly going to plan. Fear not though, Rafa had everything in hand and come the end of the season, promotion was achieved with two games still to play. And as for the title...

AUGUST

The Championship season kicked off on the banks of the River Thames with Fulham entertaining United in a live televised Friday night fixture – the first of 12 occasions the cameras would beam a Magpies fixture around the world. On a sweltering early August evening, the new-look United struggled to find any rhythm and a Matt Smith header on the stroke of half time condemned them to defeat. Huddersfield Town, who

United walk out for the season's opener at Fulham.

would prove to be the early season pacesetters, were the first visitors to Gallowgate and earned a deserved 2-1 victory with a display of hard running counter attacking football. United's new number nine, Dwight Gayle, grabbed the home side's consolation which boded well for the Londoner having opened his United account on his home debut. In a busy opening month to the season, after all there were another 44 league games to squeeze into the campaign, United were back in action four days later when another side tipped to do well, Reading, journeyed north. This time United were at their clinical best and ran out 4-1 winners. A valuable three points were picked up at Ashton Gate the following week before Chris Hughton's Brighton came to town. In front of nearly 50,000 fans, United put down a marker by beating their fellow promotion contenders 2-0 to end the month, after a very poor start, in a respectable fourth place.

SEPTEMBER

The first fixture of the month was a tough away game at Derby but a dominant United prevailed 2-0, thanks partly to a stunning volley from Yoan Gouffran. And the following midweek a rampant Magpies side put six past QPR at Loftus Road which sent shock waves around the Championship and earned Rafa the LMA

Ecstasy as Gayle's dramatic injury-time winner seals victory over Norwich.

Performance of the Week award. But just when things looked to be rolling along nicely, Wolves came north and won 2-0 at St. James' Park to send United back to earth with a bump. A point at Villa Park followed before what may be seen as one of the season's defining fixtures. Norwich led 3-1 at Gallowgate with only 21 minutes left but United were given hope when Gouffran pulled one back two minutes later. Heading into the fifth minute of injury time United were still behind and set for a damaging home defeat before, amazingly, Dwight Gayle scored twice in two minutes to turn the game completely on its head. United were elated beyond belief; the Canaries were left stunned.

OCTOBER

On the first day of the month Christian Atsu, on loan from Chelsea, scored the only goal at Rotherham before a comfortable home win over Brentford elevated United into the top two for the first time, a position they would never relinquish. A Dwight Gayle brace won the points at Barnsley, before the month was

Aleksandar Mitrovic nets his second at Deepdale.

rounded off with wins against Ipswich, 3-0 at St. James' and Preston, 2-1 at Deepdale, where Aleksandar Mitrovic stepped up to the plate to score twice to send the Geordie masses behind the goal delirious. A 15-point haul from October's five games was just the ticket for Rafa's improving side.

NOVEMBER

Cardiff became the seventh team United triumphed over, the Bluebirds losing 2-1 in Newcastle before another Gayle double saw United win 2-0 very impressively at Elland Road. Lowly Blackburn, who would be ultimately relegated, were the next team United would face with surely another three points a mere

Dwight Gayle opens the scoring at Elland Road.

certainty. But football has a habit of 'kicking you in the teeth' and the overall strength of the Championship was there for everyone to see as Rovers were worthy winners against a surprisingly out of sorts United.

DECEMBER

The month began disastrously for United as they lost 2-1 at Nottingham Forest but that wasn't the half of it. Firstly, Jonjo Shelvey was red-carded, then Matt Ritchie put United ahead before Forest missed from

Karl Darlow saves Nicklas Bendtner's penalty.

the spot or, rather, Karl Darlow saved magnificently from Nicklas Bendtner. Then Paul Dummett was dismissed for a foul in the box which afforded Forest another chance to level, but this time Henri Lansbury was denied by Darlow. Up against it with only nine men, Forest equalised early in the second half and the Magpies only fell to a late winner from the hosts. United's clear injustice was vindicated as the FA later rescinded both red cards – it didn't give them any points though! Successive victories against Birmingham, Wigan and Burton followed to steady the ship with the win at the DW Stadium being Rafa's 1000th game as a manager since starting off at Real Madrid back in 1993. Christmas and the New Year brought a win and a loss, including a 'revenge' victory over Forest, as United ended 2016 in pole position.

JANUARY

Blackburn completed the double over United in the first fixture of the New Year in a disappointing start to 2017 for the thousands of black n' whites who packed into the away end at Ewood Park. Another away fixture followed but this time, thanks to Daryl Murphy's first league goal of the season, the Magpies won

Daryl Murphy heads the winner at Griffin Park.

2-1 at Brentford. Rock bottom Rotherham completed the three-league fixture month for United and, after a shaky start, Rafa's men turned on the style to send the Millers packing back to South Yorkshire on the end of a 4-0 hammering.

FEBRUARY

There were seven games in February but an unbeaten run generating 15 points was a more than satisfactory outcome. QPR and Derby at home brought four points before a big three points were netted at Molineux. Coming from behind late on to draw at Norwich showed great character, which was followed by a home

Ayoze Pérez scores after only 23 seconds at Carrow Road.

win over Villa. Bristol City at Gallowgate only brought a point but it could have been worse as United were two down early in the game. And then the big one, away to leaders Brighton. Trailing to an early Glenn Murray penalty, it took until the 81st minute for United to draw level, somewhat fortuitously through Mo Diame. And then, sensationally, with a minute left on the clock, Matt Ritchie's raking cross-field ball found Christian Atsu on the left wing and when he delivered the ball into the box Ayoze Pérez was on hand to clinically slot past David Stockdale from 12 yards out. What a moment for Rafa and his players, not to mention the away supporters!

MARCH

There was no let up for United as third placed Huddersfield, hot on the heels of the top two, were up next. United's game plan worked a treat though and a 3-1 away success was a real tonic for United. When that was followed by an important point at Reading, the Magpies had come through their trickiest part of the season unscathed.

A very good Fulham side, who were to falter at the Play Off stage, completed the double over United in mid-March before another point was collected on the road at Birmingham.

Matt Ritchie converts from the spot at Huddersfield.

APRIL

And so to April, the month that Rafa called the most important of the season and where those that 'stood up to be counted' would be the ones to prevail. The seven game mini-season began perfectly with narrow back-to-back home wins over lowly Wigan and Burton. A defeat at Hillsborough followed before the

Jamaal Lascelles heads home against Leeds.

Geordie fans were left shell-shocked by Leeds' 95th minute equaliser in the next game at St. James' Park, and when a 3-1 defeat at Ipswich followed, United, though still looking good for promotion, were seemingly waving the Championship title goodbye as Brighton moved seven points clear at the top. A top two finish was still in United's hands though and in front of the Monday night Sky cameras, an emphatic 4-1 win over Preston secured their Premier League place. With Brighton incredibly losing to Norwich and Bristol City, and United winning at Cardiff, Albion would go into the final game of the season with a one point advantage. For the record, United's win at Cardiff was their 14th success on the road during the season, a new club high, beating the 13 wins in 2009/10.

MAY

And so to the denouement. The title was in Brighton's hands if they won at Aston Villa. If they failed to do so, a win over Barnsley at a packed and fervent St. James' Park would see the trophy being lifted by captain Jamaal Lascelles. Pérez put United ahead and come half time, with it being goalless at Villa Park,

Ayoze Pérez wheels away after opening the scoring against Barnsley.

the title was United's. Chancel Mbemba added to United's tally on the hour mark but then disaster, well, in a football sense anyway – Villa were down to ten men and Brighton had scored from the penalty spot to put them back in the box seat. Was the trophy heading south? Gayle added a third for United to seal the win but his celebrations, and the crowd's too, were a little subdued as Villa were still going into the dying embers of the game. Less than a minute later though the mood inside St. James' Park totally changed as news filtered through, in sporadic bursts, that Jack Grealish had equalised. Albion couldn't grab an injury time winner and when the full time whistle blew in the Midlands, it was met with unbounded joy on the pitch and in the stands on Tyneside. Champions, only just, but nevertheless fully deserved after a gruelling rollercoaster 46 game campaign.

125 YEARS UNITED – PART 1

The 2017/18 season marks the 125th year of Newcastle United. Here, in three separate sections in the Annual, we detail a concise history of this famous football club, decade by decade, illustrated with some tremendous archive photography.

We start here looking at the period from 1881-1919.

EAST END

Forming in 1881 from a cricket eleven, East End are originally known as Stanley before changing names in 1882. They strengthen, absorbing Rosewood FC as their reserves, and play games at Byker before a move to Chillingham Road, Heaton. East End join the new Northern League alongside city rivals, West End, in 1888.

WEST END

West End, backed by wealthy local dignitary William Neasham, form in 1882 and play their matches on a cricket pitch on the Town Moor before moving to a pitch off the Great North Road. In 1886, St. James' Park in the industrial city centre becomes their home and they march on as East End's strongest adversaries.

1890s

Newcastle becomes a one club city. East End prosper as a limited company, while West End struggle on and off the pitch. In 1892, the game is up and East End absorb their West End rivals, taking the keys for St. James' Park. A new name is chosen and on 9th December 1892, Newcastle United is born. United join the Football League in 1893 and – now wearing black and white stripes – they reach the First Division by 1898.

Andy Aitken

1900s

The fledgling club comes of age. The Edwardian Masters – Lawrence, Veitch, McCracken, Rutherford, McWilliam, Shepherd, Howie, Aitken and more – sweep opposition aside, winning the First Division title in the 1904/05 season. Another two league titles follow and United reach the FA Cup final in 1905, 1906 and 1908.

McCracken, Veitch & Howie

1910s

There's a first ever FA Cup win for the Magpies in 1910 but Britain is soon braced for war. Newcastle United's Donald Simpson Bell (left) becomes the first professional player to enlist in the army and is tragically killed in action. His incredible bravery is commended with the Victoria Cross.

continues on pages 28/29 ...

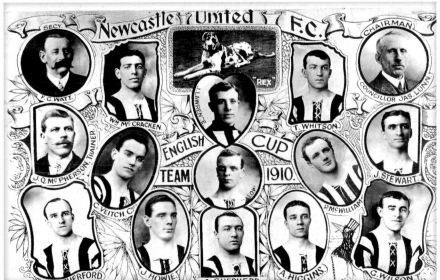

It was way back in 1875 that the first set of sporting cards was produced, with footballers appearing on the cards from the 1890s. Then, in 1906, Ogden's produced a set of football cards depicting footballers in their club colours in one of the first full-colour sets.

These cards were of course the forerunners of the hugely popular Match Attax cards that many of you collect today.

In this article we depict a few of the different cards through the ages, with a Newcastle United theme of course.

The majority of cards were produced by various Tobacco companies of the day to advertise their brand and we display a selection on the right from United's golden Edwardian era, when the Magpies won the League Championship on three occasions and appeared in five FA Cup Finals.

ANDY AITKEN – THREE NUNS

JOCK PEDDIE – OGDENS

JACK RUTHERFORD – JOHN SINCLAIR LTD

ALBERT SHEPHERD – PACKERS

JIMMY HOWIE – TADDY

BILL MCCRACKEN – F&J SMITHS

F.&J. SMITH'S CIGARETTES
NEWCASTLE UNITED.
W. McCRACKEN.

PROMINENT FOOTBALLERS.
J. HOWIE,
NEWCASTLE UNITED.

THREE NUNS TOBACCO No 21
A. AITKEN.

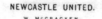
PACKER'S CHOCOLATE   SPORTS MIXTURE.
A. SHEPHERD,
NEWCASTLE UNITED.

J. H. Peddie,
Newcastle United.
Ogden's Cigarettes.

FOOTBALL FAVOURITES No 28
J. RUTHERFORD,
NEWCASTLE U.F.C.
John Sinclair Ltd
Cigarettes

Note that Aitken is featured in a smart suit and tie, as opposed to the usual football kit pose.

All these players were true United greats and household names, signified by their inclusion in the card collections.

W. LOW,
NEWCASTLE U.F.C.

J. LAWRENCE,
NEWCASTLE U.F.C.

CARRERAS CIGARETTES

J. ALLEN
NEWCASTLE U. (2ND DIV.)

Two other players of the era, goalkeeper and all-time appearance record holder Jimmy Lawrence, together with teammate Wilf Low, were featured in the Smiths Cup Tie series.

Moving on and there is a nice picture of Jack Allen from 1932, the United striker who scored twice at Wembley to help defeat Arsenal in the FA Cup Final. And from the 1950s we have Ivor Broadis featured, who is also United's oldest living player at 95 years old!

IVOR ALLCHURCH
NEWCASTLE UNITED
No. 47   INSIDE FORWARD

dick keith

NEWCASTLE UNITED
Right-back   & IRELAND

International players Ivor Allchurch (Wales) and Dick Keith (Northern Ireland) were also featured in cards produced in the late 1950s whilst ten years on, two players who would help United win the Fairs Cup in 1969 – Wyn Davies and David Craig – were included in sticker album cards.

MIKE MAHONEY

IRVING NATTRASS

In 1978 Topps produced an early set of their cards with players featured including Mick Mahoney and Irving Nattrass.

Back Page Legends
Ronnie Simpson 1951-1960

Back Page Legends
Bobby Mitchell 1949-1961

PETER BEARDSLEY

DAVID GINOLA

Merlin produced a nice selection of cards in 1995 as United went so close to winning the Premier League title, but Peter Beardsley and David Ginola had to suffer at the hands of arch rival of the day, Manchester United.

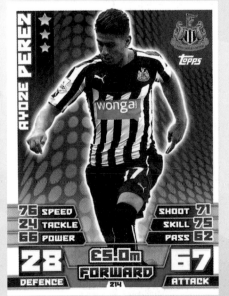

AYOZE PEREZ

wonga
Topps

76 SPEED   SHOOT 71
24 TACKLE   SKILL 75
66 POWER   PASS 62

28   £5.0m   67
DEFENCE   FORWARD   ATTACK
              214

More recently replica cards have been produced, for example the Back Page collection. Featured here, above left, are Ronnie Simpson and Bobby Mitchell, both FA Cup Winners in the 1950s, and then the Shirt of Legends series (right) which focuses on great number 9s of the past.

And back to the present, it's current midfielder Ayoze Pérez depicted in the Topps Match Attax trading card game.

SHIRT OF LEGENDS   SHIRT OF LEGENDS   SHIRT OF LEGENDS
BILL APPLEYARD   ALBERT SHEPHERD   NEIL HARRIS

SHIRT OF LEGENDS   SHIRT OF LEGENDS   SHIRT OF LEGENDS
HUGHIE GALLACHER   ALBERT STUBBINS   JACKIE MILBURN

Former Magpies

In this feature we talk to a number of former players who recount the good days they enjoyed whilst at St. James' Park.

WARREN BARTON

"I had seven great years at Newcastle and loved every minute of it. Firstly there was my debut against Coventry in August 1995. Les (Ferdinand), Shaka (Hislop) and David (Ginola) were also playing their first games and we were all blown away by the noise, passion and fervour inside the ground. We won 3-0 and it was an incredible first day in the Toon! Then there was the Man United 5-0, where it was a bit of 'payback' for us, the two Liverpool 4-3s, Barcelona and Tino's hat-trick. I also vividly recall the Forest game at the end of the 1996/97 season when the fans rejoiced in our 5-0 win, which secured Champions League football, but also loved seeing their bitter rivals Sunderland getting relegated the same afternoon.

The 8-0 over Sheffield Wednesday also sticks in my mind, not necessarily because of the score and Alan (Shearer) getting five, but because I could see Bobby (Robson) was so happy and feeling so much at home. He was a truly great football man."

KEVIN GALLACHER

"I was only at Newcastle for two seasons but during that time I quickly realised what a very special club it was. When someone like Bobby Robson comes in for you, you don't think twice and I was proud to be his first signing in the summer of 1999. The people of Newcastle were black and white in every way. They loved their football, were incredibly passionate and knew their football inside out. When you played bad they told you, but when you played well they loved you. The best memories, and ones I'll always treasure, were my last few games at home at the end of the 2000/01 season when the crowd of 52,000 gave me standing ovations for my contributions and work rate over the two seasons I was there. That's as much as you can ask for as a footballer.

As for the best game I played in, it has to be the day we beat Manchester United 3-0 at St. James' Park in December 2000. Duncan Ferguson got two and Alan (Shearer) the other. We were mid table and they were the League Champions but they couldn't match us that day and it boded well for the club over the next few seasons when Bobby took them into the Champions League."

STEVE HOWEY

"My first memory was my debut as a 19-year-old at Old Trafford in May 1989. We lost 2-0 and it was the last game of the season but it was a still a special occasion for me. And, believe it or not, I was a centre forward in my early years at the club before moving into the back four.

Then there's the Grimsby away game in the 1992/93 season when we clinched promotion, a fantastic night on and off the field and thirdly I want to mention the first home game of the 1995/96 season when we beat Coventry 3-0. We were wearing the new Adidas 'granddad collar' strips which everyone loved and the thing I remember most about the game was that virtually everyone in the crowd, which was absolutely heaving, was wearing one too. It was an incredible sight. In fact Rob Lee's excuse for having a poor game was that he kept seeing a black and white shirt on the wing and so kept passing the ball out of play to someone in the crowd!

I'm delighted too that we're wearing red numbers on the backs of the shirts this season, as we did that in my early years at the club, and I think it really adds to the 'magic' of the famous old shirt."

PETER JACKSON

"I loved my time at Newcastle United. Although we lost 2-0, my greatest memory remains my debut at Aston Villa back in October 1986. I was very nervous but pulling on the black and white shirt for the first time and playing in the first division after having spent my earlier career in the lower leagues was an unbelievable feeling which made me incredibly proud.

And then, to cap it all, I won the Player of the Year award at the end of the season. Peter Beardsley was third, Gazza was second and little old me first, can you believe it! And to follow in the footsteps of legends such as Malcolm Macdonald and Kevin Keegan is mind-blowing, it's something no one can take away from me."

ROB LEE

"Where do I start? I had 10 fantastic years at the club with so many great memories. When I signed I didn't quite realise what the club meant to everyone in the region but after making my league debut at Peterborough, I soon found out. It's a big city club and it still amazes me that the whole city is Newcastle daft. Grannies and little babies were all dressed in their black and white kits – unbelievable!

Playing in that game at London Road made me appreciate what a huge club I'd signed for, even though we were in the second tier. The fans took over the whole town and it's they who make this club so special. There were seven or eight thousand of them in the ground and they roared us to victory that afternoon. Later in the season the Grimsby and Leicester games stand out, as does our return to Europe in Antwerp, when I was fortunate enough to score a hat-trick of headers. Everyone knows how special the Manchester United and Barcelona games were in 1996 and 1997 and I just count myself so lucky to have been a part of Newcastle United during those times. We might not have won anything but we entertained a whole load of people along the way."

PETER LOVENKRANDS

"My abiding memory of my time at Newcastle was the West Brom home game in January 2009 which was just a few days after my Dad, Bent, had passed away. The support I got that night from the fans, my teammates and everyone at the club was beyond anything I could imagine, I still get goosebumps just thinking about it. And the fact that I scored in the game made it even more meaningful, especially when the announcer read out my name to confirm the goal, the reception was just incredible and really helped me get through the sadness.

It's a massive club and I was proud to play for Newcastle. When we were promoted in 2009/10 there was a fantastic bond between the players, the best I've ever known in all my years in football. We'd go out together in large groups to the cinema, or play golf, such was the friendship within the squad and I'm sure that contributed to our success.

As for one other standout moment, it was in March 2009 when I opened the scoring against Manchester United at St. James' Park and in sticking it past Edwin van der Sar, a legendary goalkeeper, it ended his 'shut-out' record. The Gallowgate End just erupted!"

MICK QUINN

"I have to go back to my debut against Leeds in August 1989 even though there was a lot of unrest in the city as we'd just been relegated. Jim Smith had just signed a centre forward from the south coast (Portsmouth) and I think I was about the 23rd choice striker in the fans' eyes! 'Sack the Board' was the cry from the fans, and 'Who's Mick Quinn?' Welcome to Newcastle I thought!

Nobody wanted the number 9 shirt as it carried such a heavy burden with the likes of Jackie Milburn and Malcolm Macdonald having worn it with such success but it didn't faze me. 'I'll wear it', I told the gaffer, "I've scored goals before and I'll do it again."

The crowd were really up for it and when we got an early penalty I grabbed the ball and stuck it in the back of the net at the Gallowgate End. We were 2-1 down at half time but in the second half I scored three more and with John Gallagher adding another we ran out 5-2 winners to kick our season off in great style. The fans certainly knew who Mick Quinn was now! Scoring goals was what I was always about, it was fulfilling, second nature, but most important was that I realised how important the club was to the fans and if I was able to put a smile back on their faces then that was good enough for me."

SCOTT SELLARS

"I'd only signed the previous month so the derby fixture at St. James' Park in April 1993, played on a soaking wet pitch, was one I was really looking forward to. It was getting quite tight at the top so the 1-0 was massive for us. And I was lucky enough to score the goal down at the Leazes End. We won a free kick just outside the box and as I took most of the set pieces, it was one I really fancied. Fortunately I was able to outwit Tony Norman in the Sunderland goal and stuck it past him in the top corner.

Then there was the Liverpool game the following season where we played as well as we ever did during my time at the club, especially in the first half where we tore them apart down the left in particular and, of course, Coley grabbed a hat-trick. With the gaffer, Peter Beardsley and Barry Venison having strong Anfield connections, the win was extra special for those lads.

My time on Tyneside brought so many happy memories, the style of football we played under Kevin (Keegan) really suited me and the fans were out of this world. As for the present, I really believe if they can get going again there's no better club in the country to be at."

STEVE WATSON

"Newcastle was my life as a youngster. After making my debut at Wolves in November 1990, and I'm still very proud to be United's youngest debutant, my home debut a few weeks later was amazing. We played Blackburn, won 1-0; all my family were there and it's an occasion I'll never forget.

Later on we had some great times with Kevin (Keegan), probably the happiest and most exciting of my career. We had a great squad, a great manager, and it was just so disappointing that we didn't win anything. Obviously the 5-0 (against Manchester United) was the highlight, but there were a few games when we knocked in seven as well.

Kenny (Dalglish) then gave us a fabulous European experience with the Barcelona game being particularly memorable. You don't often get the chance to play them, let alone beat them! All in all it was a pleasure and privilege to play for 'my team' especially at St. James' Park."

Answers on page 62.

QUIZ

What do you know about United in the past year?

1 Who did United beat last season to clinch their promotion back to the Premier League?

2 Jamaal Lascelles and Karl Darlow joined United from which club?

3 Who scored United's first and final league goals last season?

4 What was last season's average league attendance – 49,456; 51,108 or 53,223?

5 Christian Atsu plays for which African country?

6 United's Training Ground is in which Newcastle suburb – Fenham, Kingston Park or Benton?

7 Which player scored the quickest goal of the 2016/17 season against Ipswich?

8 Against which country did Freddie Woodman win his Under-20 World Cup winners' medal in May 2017?

9 Southampton manager Mauricio Pellegrino was Rafa Benítez's assistant at which of his former clubs – Inter Milan, Liverpool or Valencia?

10 If Aleksandar Mitrovic and Rob Elliot played international football against each other, who's playing?

See how much you know about United in years gone by!

1 Which country did former manager Ossie Ardiles win the World Cup with?

2 When United were last in the Premier League in 2015/16, what was the score of their final game?

3 How many times have United won the FA Cup?

4 Three United players have scored hat tricks against Sunderland – Alex Tait, Peter Beardsley and who else?

5 How many United goals did Jackie Milburn and Alan Shearer score between them – 352, 406 or 511?

6 Which of these players never played in the World Cup – Shay Given, Michael Owen, Nobby Solano or George Robledo?

7 White Hart Lane is no more but what was the score the last time United played there?

8 Kevin Keegan played for three English clubs; Scunthorpe, Liverpool and who else?

9 United's newly enlarged stadium opened at the start of which season – 1992/93, 2000/01 or 2008/09?

10 Who is the only Colombian to play for United?

FA Cup/League Cup Review

FA CUP ROUND UP

Rd 3:	Birmingham 1-1 Newcastle
Replay:	Newcastle 3-1 Birmingham
Rd 4:	Oxford 3-0 Newcastle

It was way back in 2005 that United last reached the fifth round of the FA Cup and sadly the 2016/17 season wouldn't see that poor run end. Drawn away to fellow Championship side Birmingham in Round Three, the Magpies came away from St. Andrew's with a 1-1 draw thanks to Daryl Murphy's first goal for the club. The replay, 10 days later on Tyneside, saw Gianfranco Zola's side clinically despatched by a two-goal margin.

A visit to

League One Oxford was the prize for United and in many people's eyes, an eminently winnable tie. Alas, it was the home side who triumphed against a less than full-strength Magpies outfit who, like in the 3-1 victory over Birmingham, blooded a number of Under 23s players. It might have been a different story though had Aleksandar Mitrovic not missed from the penalty spot when the score was only 1-0 to the U's – but there lies the beauty of Cup football.

LEAGUE CUP ROUND UP

Round 2:	Newcastle 2-0 Cheltenham
Round 3:	Newcastle 2-0 Wolves
Round 4:	Newcastle 6-0 Preston
Quarter Final	Hull 1-1 Newcastle
	(Hull win 3-1 on penalties)

United enjoyed a decent run in the League Cup and, for the second time in three seasons, reached the last eight of the competition. Fortunate to be handed three home draws, United knocked in ten goals without reply with the Round Four hammering of Preston being the most notable. Avoiding the 'big boys' in the Quarter Final draw, the only downside of the fixture was having to play it on Humberside with only a small allocation of tickets given to United by the home side. Dominant in the regulation 90 minutes, the Geordies failed to turn their superiority into goals but when former Tigers midfielder Mo Diame put United ahead in the 98th minute things looked rosy for the Magpies. Ignoring all the (oh so true) clichés about defending well and concentrating straight after scoring, Rafa's men immediately conceded their hard-earned advantage, Robert Snodgrass scoring and, with no more goals registered, a penalty shoot-out ensued. Newcastle, with only one competitive penalty success behind them in their entire history (a win at Watford in 2006), duly followed the form book and, in desperately disappointing circumstances, exited the competition after misses by Dwight Gayle, Jonjo Shelvey and Yoan Gouffran.

SPOT THE BALL

CAN YOU SPOT THE BALL IN THIS MATCH LAST SEASON BETWEEN NEWCASTLE AND WOLVES?

Answers on page 62

AND WHAT ABOUT IN THIS MATCH AGAINST FULHAM?

CELEBRITIES

In this feature we speak to six Newcastle United supporters who are all celebrities in their own right – and we're delighted to have them on board.

STEVE HARMISON
Durham & England Cricketer

"I'm proud to be a Newcastle United supporter and have been for as long as I can remember – I hail from Ashington where, of course, the Milburn and Charlton families are legendary figures.

One of the first games I recall was against Millwall in May 1989. Not the most glamourous you might think, but we had some family up from London so we all went together. I can still see it today, the stadium was nothing like it is today but it still had that special and unique feeling. Ando (John Anderson) hammered in a spectacular goal from distance and believe me that was a real treat as he didn't score that many. It just flew past their keeper and it's one of those memories that will just stick in your mind forever.

I was only a small lad in those days but still got a place in the School of Excellence which was hugely enjoyable and then, when I started my cricket career with Durham and progressed into the England team, Bobby Robson would invite me up to the Training Ground to help me with my fitness and conditioning. For the six years I did that, it was tremendously beneficial to my cricket and something I'll always be indebted to the club for letting me do. I got to know the players really well and formed great friendships with lads like Steve Harper (left) who were Newcastle United through and through. Happy days!"

TIM HEALY
Actor

"I was born in Benwell in the West End of Newcastle and my first memories of going down to St. James' Park were on the trolley bus, the fare was just tuppence! It was around 1959 and I thought players like Ivor Allchurch and Len White were just fantastic. They were the stand-out names and to little lads like myself going along for the first time, it was compelling stuff.

I enjoyed the 60s era which culminated in winning the Fairs Cup in 1969 and I'm fortunate that our captain that day, Bobby Moncur (below), is a good friend of mine. I loved watching the forward pairing of Wyn Davies and Pop Robson and the young lad, Alan Foggon, who was just a couple of years older than me.

I'm good friends with Mick Quinn too; he knew everything about playing centre-forward and I have to say he was the fastest player I knew over one

yard – that's why he nipped in to score so many goals.

More recently, I loved the 5-0 win over Manchester United in 1996 and as it happened, after the game, I was invited down into the Players Lounge area where I happened to be standing next to none other than Alex Ferguson. After our amazing victory, that was surreal.

My two sons, Matthew and Louis, are big fans too, as you would expect, and when Matthew is on tour (he's the lead singer and guitarist for the rock band, The 1975), more often than not he'll be wearing his black and white shirt around the venues."

LYNSEY HIPGRAVE
Broadcaster

"I've been in love with Newcastle United for as long as I can remember. The club is in my blood and has always been a part of my life, my Dad made sure of that! He used to take me and my older brother to the family enclosure when we were bairns to watch the reserves play and to watch the team train when there were open sessions under Kevin Keegan. There's nothing like the noise and passion that reverberates around St. James' Park, seeing the elation on my Dad's face when the team score and the whole place is rocking.

My favourite season was 1992/93 when we were promoted as Champions and on the final day the whole place went barmy when we beat Leicester 7-1. We saw the open top bus parade and the atmosphere was like nothing I have ever experienced. A black and white sea of delirium,

optimism and pride. A whole city united, it was intoxicating and I was hooked. It's the pride you feel in being part of the best fan-base in the world. It's sharing the hurt and pain when we lose and the ecstasy when we win with the rest of the Toon Army, an extended family. It's the floodlights, the bovril, the big bare bellies! I'm proud of my city and the football club is at the heart of that, the cathedral on the hill overlooking the town centre pulling everything and everyone together. It's been a tough, testing relationship at times but the love never wavers, it's unconditional."

GABBY LOGAN
Broadcaster

"My first Newcastle game at St. James' Park was in August 1993 to watch the visit of Spurs. I was a student at Durham University and I was at the match because I was taking the wife of Niki Papavasiliou.

Niki (below right) was a Greek Cypriot who had been signed by Kevin Keegan that summer and my Mum was his agent. Sadly, Papavasiliou's United days were over quite quickly and he went back to Greece. But I stayed. I found my club late in life because until that time I had always followed my Dad, Terry Yorath, wherever he played or managed. When I was 20 he was manager of Wales and so I was missing out on a weekly fixture, nobody to sweat over on a Saturday afternoon. Newcastle United was such an exciting club to be around, newly promoted and under Kevin Keegan and Sir John Hall it was the beating heart of the great city, how could I not fall in love?

One of my favourite memories was waking up on a Sunday morning in London in my flat when Manchester United were the opposition at St. James' Park in the Sky 4pm kick off. I had to go! I got a late flight, managed to get a ticket and arrived just in time to enjoy a fantastic 5-0 home win. I flew back with my colleagues from Sky but I didn't realise they were flying to Luton and my car was at Heathrow so I ended up getting a car to Heathrow and paying for a day's parking but I didn't care as it was one of the best days I had ever experienced.

I miss St. James' Park massively and think back to those days when I was there once or twice a week with a warm glow. But of course I still support from afar and have really enjoyed the successful Championship winning season."

JOHN McCRIRICK
Racing Pundit

"I was born and brought up in Surbiton, Surrey in the 1940s but I had an Uncle Bertie in Newcastle and he used to send food parcels down after the war. And that's why I became a Newcastle United supporter! I was proud to be a black and white and rejoice in the pleasure of seeing players like Frank Brennan, Bobby Mitchell and Jackie Milburn – real footballing heroes of that era. I remember the Robledo brothers (right) too, the first South American players to grace St. James' Park. The Cup meant so much back then and its demise in recent years really saddens me.

Later in life I'd meet the legendary Jackie at a race meeting at Gosforth Park shortly before he died, and my word, what a man. He was a God and the adulation he received from his adoring Geordie public was incredible, and this 30 years after he'd retired. They never forget their heroes on Tyneside! When I was younger I remember going along to Stamford Bridge, paying 2'6, and watching my heroes in the flesh. What an experience that was. Years later I was invited into one of the boxes

at Highbury and when the away fans spotted me they started singing 'There's only one John McCririck' and I have to say I was really amazed by that. They were 'my people' and it was just brilliant.

Sir John Hall took me on a tour of the stadium on another occasion and I was just taken aback by its splendour. I met Sir Bobby too and what a man he was. If someone was to ask you what the definition of an Englishman was, you would say Bobby Robson, and that's the best praise anyone could get.

With its history and tradition, Newcastle United is an institution. We suffer a lot with results on the pitch but one thing we never do is lose our passion and that's what makes the Geordie fans so special. Howay the Lads."

JADE THIRLWALL
Little Mix

"I have supported Newcastle United for as long as I can remember. My family are big fans so the club were always a topic of conversation when I was growing up. The first game I attended was against Everton in my teens and I went with my dad and my brother. Since that happy day I have become hooked on the team and even though I am on tour with Little Mix much of the time, I always check the results wherever I am in the world.

Whenever I go home I always try to fit in a few games and I often sit with my brother and friends in the Moncur Suite. I love meeting the young fans who come to chat to me and watching the team is so exciting. I love the buzz when we score a goal and everyone looks so happy and the atmosphere is fantastic. The last game I was able to attend was on my birthday on Boxing Day 2016 when the wonderful Bob Moncur surprised me with a Newcastle United birthday cake and I was delighted and privileged to receive it. On tour I wear my black and white whenever I get the chance – even on stage sometimes! I love wearing my Newcastle United football shirt – wherever I am it reminds me of the team I love."

Other than those we have spoken to in this feature, there are a number of other celebrities whose allegiance to Newcastle United has been well documented, for example Ant & Dec, Graeme Swann, Robson Green and Brendan Foster, and others with somewhat looser connections… They are former Prime Minister Tony Blair, boxer Chris Eubank, rock stars Brian Johnson and Sting, locally born singer Cheryl Cole, singer/songwriter James Bay, actors Brian Blessed and Jimmy Nail and even Thailand's former Prime Minister Abhisit Vejjajiva.

SPOT THE DIFFERENCE

Answers on page 62

Can you spot the ten differences in this match between Newcastle and Aston Villa?

125 YEARS UNITED – PART 2

1920s

A return to glory as United win the FA Cup at Wembley for the first time in 1924, with another league title, their fourth, following in 1927. Hughie Gallacher earns godlike status on Tyneside, smashing an incredible 143 goals in just 174 appearances between 1925 and 1930.

NEWCASTLE UNITED F.C. 1927-8.
Photo Gladstone Adams Newcastle

1930s

More FA Cup glory in 1932 as United controversially beat Arsenal 2-1 in the 'over the line' final. A first bitter taste of relegation soon follows though, and the Magpies are in distress as the clouds of war roll in. Former player Stan Seymour (right) joins the board to lead the recovery.

1940s

Wartime football arrives and legends of the game – Tom Finney, Bill Nicholson, Stan Mortensen – make guest appearances in black and white.

But Wallsend-born Albert Stubbins (above) eclipses them all with his sensational goalscoring as a budding local forward called Jackie Milburn watches on. The Magpies are promoted in 1948.

1950s

The Cup Kings. Mitchell dazzles, Robledo grafts, Milburn stars and captain Harvey lifts the famous old trophy. A golden era for Newcastle United, who win the FA Cup at Wembley three times in just five years – 1951, 1952 and 1955.

1960s

Relegation in 1961, promotion in 1965 (right) and European glory in the summer of '69. The decade ends in joy for Joe Harvey's flying Magpies, with captain Bobby Moncur bringing home the Fairs Cup after United vanquish Feyenoord, Sporting Lisbon, Real Zaragoza, Vitoria Setúbal, Glasgow Rangers and finally Hungarian side Ujpest Dozsa – all over two legs.

continues on pages 40/41 ...

THE 'NEW' ST JAMES' PARK

Permission to increase the capacity of St James' Park from around 36,000 to over 52,000 was granted in 1998 and, throughout 1999 and into 2000, a new seating tier on top of the existing Milburn and Leazes End stands was constructed. It was a huge task but one that was successfully completed in time for the first home game of the 2000/01 season against Derby County. Here, we illustrate how the building work progressed and it makes fascinating viewing.

CROATIA ZAGREB 2 – 2 NEWCASTLE UNITED

CHAMPIONS LEAGUE QUALIFYING ROUND, SECOND LEG
Wednesday 27th August 1997, Maksimir Stadium, Zagreb

Back in May 1997 United beat Nottingham Forest 5-0 at St. James' Park to finish in second place in the Premier League. In those days only the League Champions (Manchester United) went straight into the Group Stages, with the second-placed team progressing into the Qualifying Round. United were paired with Croatia Zagreb and in the first leg at St. James' Park they won 2-1 with a brace from John Beresford. However, the away goal scored by Zagreb made the Croatians favourites as United made the trip to Eastern Europe – and what a night it would turn out to be.

Goalless until a minute before the interval, United grabbed a priceless away goal themselves. Jon Dahl Tomasson tumbled under the challenge of Goran Jurić in the penalty area and Tino Asprilla slammed home the resultant spot kick with Jurić also seeing red. The home side were well on top in the second half and an equaliser duly arrived on the hour when a left-wing free kick was swung over by Cvitanović and headed home by Šimić at the far post. Still ahead in the final minutes, and heading through on a 3-2 aggregate, United were left stunned and undone by their own shortcomings when Alessandro Pistone lost possession to Cvitanović who beat Shay Given from the edge of the box. So, a repeat of the first leg score and extra time ahead. With few chances in added time and with the clock ticking over to 119 minutes, David Batty intercepted a ball midway inside the Croatian half. He played it into Asprilla on the edge of the home penalty box and, when the Colombian laid it off to Temuri Ketsbaia, he kept his cool to beat keeper Dražen Ladić from 10 yards. Such drama and unbridled delight amongst players and supporters – United were in the Champions League proper!

Manager Kenny Dalglish went on to say, "I've been involved in one or two games that have been decided in the last minute, but never one where it's happened twice. It was certainly a good time for Temuri to score his first goal for Newcastle! It was a Herculean effort in the first half and, even after they equalised at 1-1, we had chances to finish them off when they were down to ten men. Sometimes you need a little bit of luck in football, but they were pretty happy in the dressing room afterwards."

United:	Given, Watson, Pistone, Albert, Pearce (Howey), Batty, Lee, Barton, Asprilla, Tomasson (Ketsbaia), Beresford (Gillespie)
Goals:	Asprilla 44 pen, Ketsbaia 120
Attendance:	34,000

With the drama of the last day win over Barnsley still fresh in our minds – a result that brought the Championship title to Tyneside, with a little help from Aston Villa's Jack Grealish of course – we go back in time to relive two games that had incredible drama right at death and both with positive outcomes for Newcastle United.

FEYENOORD 2 – 3 NEWCASTLE UNITED
CHAMPIONS LEAGUE GROUP STAGE
Wednesday 13th November 2002, De Kuip, Rotterdam

United had lost their first three group games but, having won games four and five, they travelled to Holland seeking to be the first team to qualify from a group having lost their first three matches. To do so they would have to beat a team who had already won 1-0 at St. James' Park and hope that Dynamo Kiev didn't beat Juventus in the other group game being played at the same time.

And so to the game. On the stroke of half time an Alan Shearer flick found Craig Bellamy tightly marked in the box, but he was still able to stroke the ball past Lodewijks into the opposite corner of the goal. United were in heaven four minutes into the second half when a flowing move found Kieron Dyer in space down the right. He was quickly closed down by defenders but spotted Hugo Viana in space on the left edge of the box. The Portuguese midfielder took a controlling touch before hitting a firm shot with the outside of his left boot into the far corner of the goal. Goalkeeper Lodewijks got his fingers to the shot but was unable to keep it out. It was looking good for United but, with 25 minutes left, home substitute Mariano Bombarda was played in through the middle by Kalou and tucked the ball past a helpless Given from 15 yards. The momentum shifted back completely in the Feyenoord camp when, six minutes later, Dyer gave the ball away and Anthony Lurling crashed home a Kalou pass from the edge of the box. United desperately sought a winner and their efforts were miraculously rewarded in the final minute. A long ball forward from Nikos Dabizas was flicked on by Shearer to Dyer and with a lovely feint the England man was through on goal. He opted to place the ball to the keeper's left and Lodewijks was able to tip the ball away but was grounded in the process. Time stood still as the ball trickled to the side with Bellamy favourite to get there first. The Welshman hit a firm shot that hit the scrambling keeper on the legs and went inside the near post to spark scenes of unconfined joy around the Toon-supporting globe with news of Juventus' win in Kiev filtering through.

Manager Bobby Robson said, "I thought the way we played against Juventus was a great night – if we hadn't won that night, we wouldn't have been here to do that, so yes, I guess it is (greatest night as United manager).

"We never gave it up but we didn't think we'd get nine points from three games, so it's worked out wonderfully well, and Juventus have done us a great job. I'm pretty ecstatic – but I'm pretty numb as well. It's hard to believe we've won it in the end although, at one stage, we were comfortably winning it and looking as though it wouldn't be too much of a problem for us. I heard at one stage it was 1-1 in Kiev, but this game had too much in it for me to think about another game. I couldn't take in two games at the same time, so I gave that one up. We heard the score from Kiev after the final whistle, and they were ecstatic."

United:	Given, Griffin, Hughes, Dabizas, O'Brien, Speed, Jenas, Dyer, Shearer, Bellamy, Viana (Bernard)
Goals:	Bellamy 45, 90, Viana 49
Attendance:	44,500

HAT TRICK HEROES

By the time you read this, the figure of Premier League hat tricks scored by Newcastle United players may have risen from 13 to 14! Georginio Wijnaldum scored the last, against Norwich in October 2015 with club legend Peter Beardsley having the honour of hitting the first in United's inaugural Premier League season of 1993/94.

And those 13 hat tricks have been scored by ten different players. We chart them here in chronological order.

PETER BEARDSLEY v WIMBLEDON at ST. JAMES' PARK
1993/94

Beardsley didn't complete his transfer back to United until September and the following month bagged a hat trick in a 4-0 win.

ANDY COLE v LIVERPOOL at ST. JAMES' PARK
1993/94

One of United's best performances of the season, they ripped into the Merseysiders with Cole scoring his treble in the first half.

ANDY COLE v COVENTRY CITY at ST. JAMES' PARK
1993/94

Cole and Beardsley were on fire and another three for the goal machine helped United to a 4-0 success.

LES FERDINAND v WIMBLEDON at ST. JAMES' PARK
1995/96

Vinnie Jones ended up in goal for the Dons as United ran the Londoners ragged winning 6-1.

ALAN SHEARER v LEICESTER CITY at ST. JAMES' PARK
1996/97

3-1 down with 13 minutes to play, Shearer sensationally struck three times, the last in the final minute, to earn United a 4-3 victory.

ALAN SHEARER v SHEFFIELD WEDNESDAY at ST. JAMES' PARK
1999/00

In Bobby Robson's first home game, Shearer bagged five as United put eight past the Owls.

MICHAEL OWEN v WEST HAM UNITED at UPTON PARK

2005/06

Owen scored United's first Premier League hat trick on the road as United ran out 4-2 winners in East London.

ANDY CARROLL v ASTON VILLA at ST. JAMES' PARK

2010/11

Newly promoted United put six past Villa keeper Brad Friedel in their first home game of the season.

KEVIN NOLAN v SUNDERLAND at ST. JAMES' PARK

2010/11

Nolan became the third Magpie to hit a derby day hat trick, following in the footsteps of Alex Tait and Peter Beardsley.

LEON BEST v WEST HAM at ST. JAMES' PARK

2010/11

Five goals against the Hammers for United with frontman Best putting on a tremendous show in a United shirt with his treble.

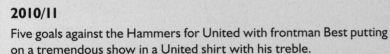

DEMBA BA v BLACKBURN ROVERS at ST. JAMES' PARK

2011/12

Six games into the season and unbeaten United despatched Rovers 3-1 on Tyneside to maintain their good start to the campaign.

DEMBA BA v STOKE CITY at THE BRITANNIA STADIUM

2011/12

Two hat tricks from Demba in five games as this time United won 3-1 in the Potteries to move third in the table.

GEORGINIO WIJNALDUM v NORWICH CITY at ST. JAMES' PARK

2015/16

A 6-2 win for United with Wijnaldum grabbing four for the Magpies, their first win of the season.

FOOTBALL MAGAZINES WITH A MAGPIES CONNECTION

Football magazines have been around for as long as we can remember with today's offerings of **MATCH** and **MATCH OF THE DAY** probably being the most popular amongst the younger generation. Full of colour, great action pictures and up-to-the-minute news, they fit the market place perfectly.

But if you're a youngster reading this ask your Dad, or even your Grandad, about the magazines he used to read back in the day when football was only broadcast once a week on television, and sometimes in black and white – imagine that!

The first football magazine came out in 1951 and was entitled **CHARLES BUCHAN'S FOOTBALL MONTHLY**; Charles being a former captain of England.

WORLD SOCCER was the second oldest monthly football magazine when it started in October 1960 and is today the longest-running magazine providing a very authoritative read. Also in the Sixties was **SOCCER STAR** which in 1968 featured a great picture of Frank Clark (standing in for regular skipper Bob Moncur) shaking hands with West

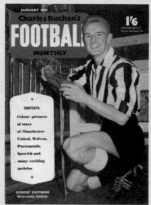

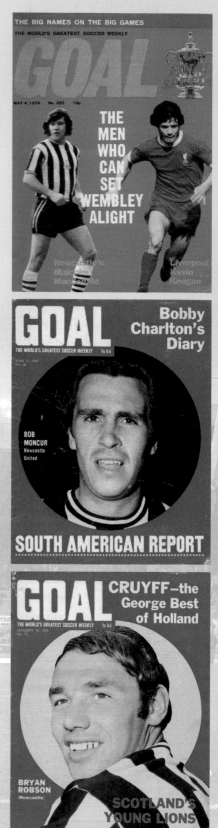

Ham's World Cup-winning captain Bobby Moore.

JIMMY HILL'S FOOTBALL WEEKLY

launched in 1967, followed by **GOAL** magazine in 1968. A year later the hugely popular **SHOOT** magazine hit the streets and by 1971 Shoot and Goal were the market leaders. Shoot had star players as weekly columnists (e.g. Bobby Moore, Billy Bremner and Kevin Keegan) and they provided a great insight into the game for younger readers. In 1979 **MATCH** was launched as competition to Shoot (which had incorporated Goal) and **MATCH OF THE DAY** followed in 2009.

TIGER AND SCORCHER

(a merger of the two comics) was a fantastic read in the early 1970s featuring the exploits of Roy of the Rovers (Roy Race of Melchester Rovers) who featured in the comic – a real boyhood hero. There was also Hot Shot Hamish, the story of a Scottish centre forward who, believe or not, packed a dynamic shot in his boots and, finally, many people's favourite, **BILLY'S BOOTS**.

This was the story of a schoolboy (Billy Dane) who acquired a pair of football boots once used by the legendary Dead Shot Kean, and it enabled Billy – an ordinary player without this special pair of boots – to become an outstanding player when he was wearing the boots.

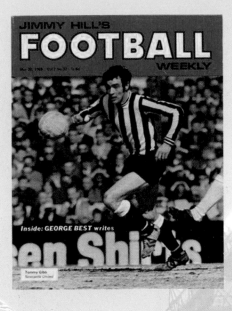

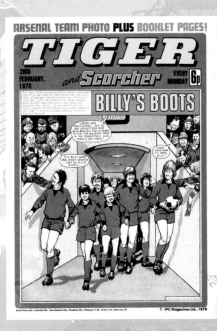

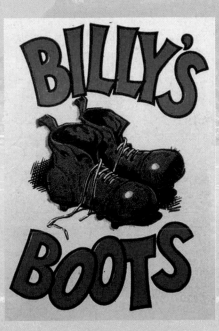

The stories each week were tremendously enjoyable and children would eagerly look forward to each Saturday morning, when the comic was published, to read the next instalment of Billy's life.

Many a time Billy would lose the boots somewhere, find them in the nick of time, and proceed to score a brilliant hat-trick in the local Schools Cup Final. During the summer months, Billy incredibly managed to get hold of a pair of Kean's cricket boots too, which did the same for him on the cricket field. Such was his standing in the game, **ROY OF THE ROVERS** also came out as a magazine by itself in the mid-1970s.

For the older readers there was little competition for World Soccer so when **WHEN SATURDAY COMES** came out in 1986, it evolved into Britain's only current independent football magazine.

90 MINUTES arrived in October 1990 and ran for seven years during which time **FOUR FOUR TWO** launched in September 1994 – and is still going strong today. **BACK PASS** is a retro magazine which has great nostalgic articles whilst **FOOTBALL KICK** is in the Match category.

So there you have it; a fantastic array of comics, magazines and fictional football heroes mixed in with the stars of today and yesteryear.

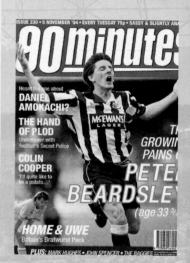

CROSSWORD

ACROSS

2 Nicknamed Sarge, striker from the 80s (7)
4 French loanee from 1999 (4)
6 Defender signed from Rangers (8)
9 Ex-midfielder, now Bury manager (5)
12 Our youngest debutant, Steve (5)
14 Greek midfielder from 1998 (10)
16 Charles the Frenchman (7)
18 Manager 1997/8 (8)
19 Keeper Rob (6)
20 Signed from Ipswich in 1999 (4)

DOWN

1 Our Ghanaian winger (4)
3 Nikos the Greek (7)
5 Midfielder, Billy from 1990 (5)
7 Spurs manager 1998-2001, George (6)
8 Big Frank, 1950s centre half (7)
10 Mehdi (5)
11 Spanish striker signed in 2008, the X-man (5)
13 Missed the target, so have another go (3,5)
15 Scottish midfielder, 1998-2001 (5)
17 Jim, 1965 Promotion winner (4)

Answers on page 62.

125 YEARS UNITED – PART 3

AND HERE WE CONCLUDE WITH THE PERIOD FROM THE 1970s TO THE PRESENT DAY.

1970s

A rollercoaster for the Magpies. Jimmy Smith, Terry Hibbitt and Tony Green all wow in black and white, while Malcolm Macdonald joins in 1971 and breaks nets – and hearts – in swaggering style. FA Cup and League Cup final heartbreak comes and goes in 1974 and 1976 and 'Supermac' moves on before United are relegated once more.

1980s

Kevin Keegan sensationally joins in 1982 and departs a hero after promotion to the top flight two years later. United introduce Beardsley's brilliance, Waddle's wing wizardry and the midfield magnificence of Gazza, but the local heroes are rich pickings for the elite and the Magpies are no longer at the top of the tree come the end of the Eighties.

1990s

Under the ownership of Sir John Hall, St. James' Park is transformed in every sense. Kevin Keegan returns as manager and from the depths of the second tier,

the Entertainers era begins in earnest. Soon, there's touching distance of Premier League titles, Albert's chip – absolutely glorious, Tino's hat-trick and, of course, the return of two of the North East's favourite sons, Alan Shearer and Sir Bobby Robson.

2000s

Sir Bobby navigates the Magpies to the upper reaches of the Premier League, earning Champions League qualification in the process, but his reign comes to an end in 2004. In 2006, Alan Shearer retires as United's and the Premier League's record goal-scorer. The football world mourns Sir Bobby's passing in 2009. Despite relegation that same summer, Chris Hughton assembles a team that will bounce straight back as Championship winners.

2010s

A fifth-place finish under Alan Pardew in 2012 sees the club return to European football but the joy is short-lived. The Magpies are relegated by 2016 but go down with optimism as Rafa Benítez commits his future. The Spaniard duly delivers and Newcastle United win the Championship title in dramatic fashion. The club will play Premier League football in its 125th anniversary year.

THE BLACK AND WHITE STRIPES

The story of Newcastle United's famous black and white stripes is a fascinating one, so read on…

1884

NEWCASTLE UNITED

1891

NEWCASTLE UNITED

1894

NEWCASTLE UNITED

After changing from East End's red colours for the first two decades of Newcastle United's history, the Club saw their side wear dark blue shorts, not black, in many games up to the First World War.

And in the years leading to the hostilities, United pulled on a shirt with broad stripes featured on the front and back of the jersey. It was the start of a remarkable series of differing designs of black and white stripes.

1910

NEWCASTLE UNITED

Hughie Gallacher, 1926/27

1930

NEWCASTLE UNITED

In the twenties the stripes became narrower, while centre stripes varied from white to black. Generally though, the club shirt remained the same right up to season 1958-59, with the exception of a change in collar from the 'grandad' look to a conventional one.

However, with Charlie Mitten installed as boss in 1958, his modern and continental influence gave the black n' white a dramatic change. In came a streamlined version, but few liked it in an era of traditional values.

The kit was perhaps a decade ahead of its time and was rapidly shelved, to be replaced by a more conventional style for the sixties. It was rare for the club to show any crest on the shirt up to then, apart from in FA Cup Finals.

1955 FA Cup Final

1958

NEWCASTLE UNITED

Moncur and Macdonald 1972

During the following decade, kit manufacturers started to play a major part in football. A succession of companies like Bukta, Umbro and Asics started to find imaginative ways of designing United's classical black n' white striped shirt using logos, side flashes, different styles of collars, and the introduction of blue tints as United's third colour.

And with the introduction of a club sponsor, the Magpies had Newcastle Breweries' famous Blue Star emblazoned on the shirt from season 1982-83, replaced by new sponsors Greenalls, then the colourful NTL: logo and afterwards the distinctive Northern Rock banner.

NEWCASTLE UNITED

Season 1989-90 saw probably the most unusual design when a mix of narrow and broad black and white stripes produced a 'bar code' look that took a while to get used to.

Adidas were United's kit manufacturer as well as official sponsor from 1995-2010 before current kit partners, Puma, took over the design and production of the world-famous Newcastle United kit producing a succession of quality designed strips.

NEWCASTLE UNITED

For the 2017-18 season the shirt includes a gold and silver commemorative crest to mark the club's 125th football season, based on the city's coat of arms, as well as the logo of new sponsors Fun88. Furthermore, the kit features red numbers for the first time since the 1992-93 season.

It is quite amazing what can be done with black and white stripes!

THE UNITED CREST

The present crest of Newcastle United was first used during season 1988-89 after the club had occasionally, over the years, displayed on their shirts the City of Newcastle upon Tyne coat of arms, specifically for those Cup Finals, although it appears that for the club's earliest finals – 1905, 1906 and 1908 – United did not display any crest; 1910 being the first final with any badge on their shirt.

The two mythical seahorses on either side are a reminder of Newcastle's seaport heritage, whilst the crest that was worn for the first 80 years of United's history carried the motto, *Fortiter Defendit Triumphans* – Triumphing by Brave Defence.

SUMMARY

SEASON	KIT MANUFACTURER	PERIOD	SHIRT SPONSOR
1974-1975	Bukta	1980-1986	Newcastle Breweries
1975-1976	Umbro	1986-1990	Greenall's Beers
1976-1980	Bukta	1990-2000	McEwan's Lager/
1980-1993	Umbro		Newcastle Brown Ale
1993-1995	Asics	2000-2003	NTL:
1995-2010	Adidas	2003-2012	Northern Rock
2010-current	Puma	2012-2013	Virgin Money
		2013-2017	Wonga
		2017-date	Fun88

UNITED in the COMMUNITY

Newcastle United Foundation is the official charity of Newcastle United Football Club. It uses the local passion for football to inspire, encourage learning and promote healthy lifestyles, making a real difference to the lives of children, young people and families in the North East region.

Through its health, community, education and coaching programmes, the Foundation has worked with almost 50,000 people across Newcastle, Gateshead, North Tyneside and Northumberland in the last year.

Here are a few pictures of some of the projects from last season together with a number of other activities and events, including linking up with commercial partners, which the players were involved with as part of their commitment to support the local community.

GIRLS DEVELOPMENT SQUAD

Ayoze Pérez was pleased to attend one of the Under-9 Girls Development Squad training sessions at the first-team Training Centre. Pérez joined in with drills and skills training as well as giving his advice to the girls, all of whom listened attentively, in a fun-filled evening. This visit inspired Ayoze to sign up as a Foundation Ambassador and he went on to support the Foundation throughout the season.

BRAVEHEARTS

Karl Darlow attended the annual Bravehearts Awards at St. James' Park where 33 children received awards and gifts from Karl and BBC Look North presenter Carol Malia. Bravehearts is a charity that recognises the courage and bravery in children, many of whom have undergone major operations at the city's Royal Victoria Infirmary. It proved to be a delightful, rewarding and uplifting experience for Karl.

WORLD ORPHAN DAY

Christian Atsu visited a Foundation Soccer School to raise awareness of World Orphan Day and the charity 'Arms Around the Child'. Christian joined in with the training session before telling the youngsters about his experience supporting an orphanage in Ghana. The children donated some kit on behalf of the Foundation and Newcastle United Academy for Christian to take back to the orphans he supports.

FOUNDATION FAMILY CELEBRATION

Rob Elliot joined over 300 children and families to celebrate their graduation from Newcastle United Foundation's Family Learning programme at St. James' Park. Family Learning is an after-school club for children and their parents/guardians that aims to help participants become stronger, healthier families while also aiming to give participating adults the confidence to explore further learning.

BT DISABILITY FUND

Players from Newcastle United Foundation's Frame Football Club met Yoan Gouffran and Vurnon Anita to launch the BT and Premier League's Disability Fund, which aims to inspire even more disabled people to become more active and develop new skills and confidence. The Foundation's Disability teams include Down's Syndrome, Cerebral Palsy, Amputee, Frame, Deaf, Visually-Impaired, Blind and Power Chair teams.

WEST END FOODBANK

Isaac Hayden lent his support to the Newcastle West End Foodbank which opened in 2013 and is now the largest in the UK, with up to 1000 people (adults and children) receiving a food parcel each week. United supporters donated several tonnes of food on matchdays last season which significantly beefed up the foodbank stocks. The enthusiasm Isaac brought on his visit helped cheer many vulnerable people throughout the city.

KICKS

Rafa Benítez and Jamaal Lascelles paid a surprise visit to the Foundation's Premier League Kicks session at Westgate Community College in the west end of Newcastle. They met over 200 of the participants and watched them in action under the floodlights. The atmosphere was electric and aside from the youngsters, it was also an unforgettable experience for the Manager and Captain!

TESCO BANK

The Tesco Bank Junior Players programme was launched by Ayoze Pérez, Sunderland AFC's Duncan Watmore, and Newcastle Eagles' Fab Flournoy. The community sports programme sees 15,000 primary school pupils from across the North East take part in football and basketball sessions led by the Newcastle United Foundation, the Foundation of Light and Newcastle Eagles Community Foundation.

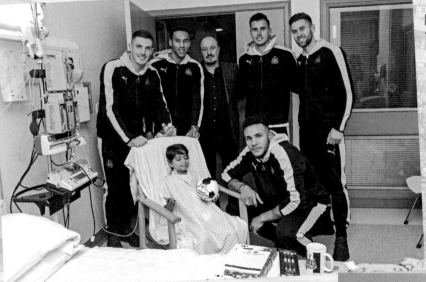

HOSPITALS

The visit to the local Newcastle hospitals is one of the highlights of the year for both the United players and staff as well as the children they meet whilst visiting the wards, where they aim to bring some festive cheer to the children who are unfortunate enough to be hospitalised during the Christmas period. The Royal Victoria Infirmary, which houses the Great North Children's Hospital, is the main beneficiary of the visit and they also receive a cash donation from the players.

SHOW RACISM THE RED CARD

Newcastle United continue to be one of the foremost supporters of the SRtRC Charity and in one of two workshops held at St. James' Park during the season, Karl Darlow and Yoan Gouffran met over 100 local school children offering words of advice and support about tackling racism in football and society. Pictured also is former United player Olivier Bernard with representatives of the Women's football team.

Wordsearch

Tackle the clues and find the answers in the grid. Words can go horizontally, vertically and diagonally in all eight directions.

```
E J K X J B Q G R U C N O M T L L
X L M I L B U R N Q D B Z M Y I N
E N V B S M N K V N A C Z P N V Y
T Z Y G T O Q Q V L G T A E Y B A
E K N T D B U F E P X N K S Q L D
R W X V L M Y T H T O E E B T A S
P E F P B M P D H D R L L Z F C E
L M F Q A T A R A A L J Y R N I N
K B F L M R D R B E M B A T L M D
S L L B C J A T C E B P G R R E E
D E T H K M R S H G A Y T J D D W
B Y Z S H V A V V W W R T O T A Z
X P D A R L M G X R T L D N N C M
T Q W M E U T M X R F D B S R A F
Z N M M Y L H R K M L G D V L N Z
D V L K O N I T T E H C O P Z E L
D L A N O D C A M M L O C L A M Y
```

United's number nine (5)
Argentina great from 1986 World Cup (8)
2022 World Cup hosts (5)
Losing League Cup Finalists 2017 (11)
The home of football (stadium) (7)
Team name which is a day of the week (9)
Welsh Champions League winner (4)
Fairs Cup captain 1969 (6)
Opposite the Gallowgate End (6)
Supermac (7/9)

Club captain in 2016/17 (9)
Wor Jackie (7)
Nicknamed Pedro (9)
The other St. James' Park (6)
Tottenham boss (10)
Match of the Day host (7)
World Cup Final hat trick man (5)
Hamilton from Scotland (10)
Played alongside Shearer from 2001-05 (7)
United's Chilean brothers (7)

Answers on page 62.

Newcastle United   **47**

THE BEST GOALS OF 2016/17

DWIGHT GAYLE v READING at ST. JAMES' PARK, 17 AUGUST 2016

United needed a win to get their season up and running and on 69 minutes, and defending a slender 2-1 advantage, Dwight Gayle stepped up to seal the points for the Magpies. Isaac Hayden saw a forward run halted illegally, which afforded Gayle the opportunity to hammer in a fabulous 25-yard free kick from a central area past a helpless Ali Al-Habsi; a stunning effort from United's new number 9.

DWIGHT GAYLE v BRISTOL CITY at ASHTON GATE, 20 AUGUST 2016

Just before the mid-point of the first half, Chancel Mbemba won the ball in his own half and played it forward to Mo Diame. The Senegal midfielder played an inch perfect pass to Dwight Gayle whose control at pace, and finish with his second touch, were immaculate. It was enough to win the game and earn United their first away points of the season. If his Reading goal was stunning, this was clinical.

YOAN GOUFFRAN v DERBY COUNTY at PRIDE PARK, 10 SEPTEMBER 2016

Following a two-week break for international fixtures, United were on the road once again. After a deflected shot from Dwight Gayle won Newcastle a corner kick at the 'home' end of the ground, Jonjo Shelvey hit a long deep corner away from the 'big lads' around the penalty spot, where Yoan Gouffran was on hand to majestically smash home a superbly timed volley past Scott Carson. No one would hit a sweeter volley all season.

JONJO SHELVEY v QPR at LOFTUS ROAD, 13 SEPTEMBER 2016

Four days on from picking up three points at Derby, United earned their third successive away win, this time an unprecedented 6-0 win at Loftus Road. Already two up and totally bossing the game, Jonjo Shelvey's second of the game saw the United playmaker hit an unstoppable effort from 25 yards that simply flew into the top corner past a stationary Alex Smithies. A rocket from the England midfielder.

CHRISTIAN ATSU v ROTHERHAM UNITED at THE NEW YORK STADIUM, 1 OCTOBER 2016

Jonjo Shelvey, whose telling contributions from the middle of the park were crucial to United's success, found Christian Atsu on the right wing and the Chelsea loanee, now a permanent member of Rafa's squad, beat his man before curling a shot beyond Lee Camp into the far corner of the net in front of the North Stand. It would be the first of five goals for the Ghanaian winger, and a real classy finish.

AYOZE PÉREZ v IPSWICH TOWN at ST. JAMES' PARK, 22 OCTOBER 2016

Just 58 seconds! A fantastic start to the game saw all eleven Magpies, including goalkeeper Karl Darlow, touch the ball and none of the opposition make contact with it – until Town goalkeeper Bartosz Bialkowski fished the ball out of the Leazes End net. Jonjo Shelvey's crossfield ball to Paul Dummett was the 19th pass of the sequence, allowing the left back to centre with the 20th, Yoan Gouffran flicked it on before Ayoze Pérez hit a controlled volley from just outside the six-yard box. The perfect team goal.

DWIGHT GAYLE v NOTTINGHAM FOREST at ST. JAMES' PARK, 30 DECEMBER 2016

The scores were level at 1-1 just after the hour mark when Dwight Gayle pursued a diagonal cross from Ciaran Clark in hope rather than expectation. But then Eric Lichaj's attempted header back towards his keeper dropped into the number nine's path and he powered home a right-footed effort from the narrowest of angles. Opportunism at its best.

AYOZE PÉREZ v BRIGHTON & HOVE ALBION at AMEX STADIUM, 28 FEBRUARY 2017

This was a huge game and with the score tied at 1-1 and only a minute to go, United struck. Having switched wings with Christian Atsu, Matt Ritchie produced a superb cross-field ball from inside his own half on the right to his Ghanaian colleague. Atsu tamed the ball before pinging it across the box for Ayoze Pérez to hammer home clinically and magically from 12 yards. The coolest of executions.

MATT RITCHIE v BURTON ALBION at ST. JAMES' PARK, 5 APRIL 2017

Things were getting a bit tight at the top and a home win was much needed. Goalless after 68 minutes, Jonjo Shelvey, occupying a central midfield position just over halfway, played a pass forward to Matt Ritchie in the middle of a quartet of opposing players. He strode towards the penalty area before unleashing an unstoppable right-footed shot into the Leazes End goal. A special moment from the magic man.

CHRISTIAN ATSU v CARDIFF CITY at THE CARDIFF CITY STADIUM, 28 APRIL 2017

Needing a win to have any hope of lifting the Championship trophy, Daryl Murphy combined with Ayoze Pérez to feed Christian Atsu on the edge of the Cardiff box and, as he shaped to shoot, Sean Morrison collided with him inside the 'D' at the expense of a free-kick. Atsu took one stride before nonchalantly chipping the ball over the wall and into the top corner past a motionless Allan McGregor. An exquisite strike.

AYOZE PÉREZ v BARNSLEY at ST. JAMES' PARK, 7 MAY 2017

United needed a win to put the pressure on leaders Brighton and they got off the mark in fine style through Ayoze Pérez's 11th goal of the season. Jonjo Shelvey swept a fine first time pass out to Christian Atsu down the Newcastle right. The winger came inside before back-heeling the ball to DeAndre Yedlin who crossed to the near post for Pérez to supply a fabulous flick that beat goalkeeper Adam Davies in the Leazes End goal.

ST. JAMES' PARK –
MORE THAN JUST NEWCASTLE UNITED

Most of you will know that St. James' Park is more than just a football stadium hosting Newcastle United. Aside from hosting many conference and banqueting events on a daily basis, as well as such events as the **X Factor** auditions, it's the pitch itself that is the focus of this article as we detail below a number of other events, together with some great imagery, that have taken place on the hallowed turf.

Euro '96

OTHER SPORTING EVENTS OF NOTE

EURO 96, HOST TO THREE GROUP PHASE GAMES

OLYMPIC FOOTBALL 2012

RUGBY LEAGUE MAGIC WEEKEND 2015, 2016, 2017

THE RUGBY WORLD CUP 2015

The Match

GOAL!

Olympic Football

The two most notable football occasions were the Euro 96 group games and the 2012 Olympic Football matches. Back in 1996 France, Romania and Bulgaria were the three teams who played at St James' Park with the fourth team in Group B, Spain, playing all three of their games in Leeds.

And then in 2012, six games in the Men's Tournament and three in the Women's were staged on Tyneside. The stand-out game was probably the Men's Quarter Final between Brazil and Honduras, which the five time World Cup winners won 3-2 with goals from Damião (2) and Neymar.

There have also been seven full England International games played at St. James' Park, the most recent being England v Azerbaijan in 2005, together with numerous 'B', Under 21 and representative matches.

CONCERTS

1982 – THE ROLLING STONES

1984 – BOB DYLAN

1985 – BRUCE SPRINGSTEEN

1986 – QUEEN

1990 – THE ROLLING STONES

2006 – BRYAN ADAMS

2007 – ROD STEWART

2014 – KINGS OF LEON

The Rolling Stones

MISCELLANEOUS

GOAL, THE 2005 FOOTBALL DRAMA FILM WHICH GAVE A CAMEO ROLE TO ALAN SHEARER.

SKY ONE'S 'THE MATCH' REACHED ITS CONCLUSION IN FRONT OF NEAR FULL HOUSES IN 2004, 2005 AND 2006.

Even before and after World War Two, track and field and cycling events took place at the stadium. There was also boxing in 1916, baseball in 1944 – when a US Navy team played a US Army team in a wartime exhibition game – whilst the famous Harlem Globetrotters basketball team entertained the Tyneside public in the 1950s.

Bizarrely, sheep-dog trials have even been staged on the pitch whilst St. James' Park has also been used as a location for film and television programmes.

There was also a Royal visit to the stadium in 1917 when HM King George V and Queen Mary arrived for an investiture and decoration presentation.

Rod Stewart

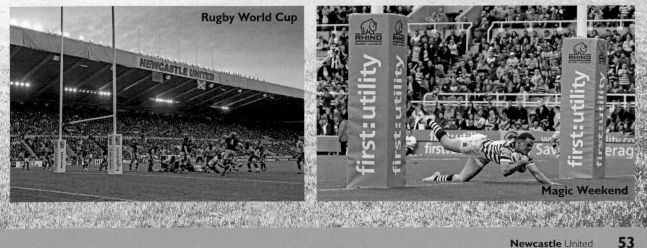
Rugby World Cup

Magic Weekend

ISAAC HAYDEN

Boyhood hero?
Patrick Vieira

Best footballing moment?
Promotion last season

Toughest opponent?
David Silva

Team supported as a boy?
Arsenal

Pre-match meal?
Chicken and pasta

Any superstitions?
Say a little prayer as I walk onto the pitch

Favourite current player?
Sergio Busquets

Favourite other sports person?
Daniel Ricciardo

Favourite stadium other than St James' Park?
Emirates

What would you be if you weren't a footballer?
A Director of Football role

Where did you go for your 2017 summer holiday?
Dubai and New York

What do you like in particular about the city of Newcastle?
The people, [they are] very welcoming

Favourite Actor?
Leonardo DiCaprio

Favourite TV Show?
Power

Favourite music artist/last concert seen?
Drake

What do you like doing in your spare time?
Rest and gym work

Best friend in football?
Hector Béllerín

Which three people would you invite round for dinner?
Floyd Mayweather, Kelly Brook, Sir Alex Ferguson

What's the best thing about being a footballer?
Doing what you enjoy every day

Which boots do you wear?
Puma One

What's the best goal you've scored?
Newcastle's second at Cardiff in April 2017

Favourite football show on TV?
Soccer AM

Favourite football commentator/football pundit?
Andy Gray

Favourite PS4 or Xbox game?
Tekken 7

Q and A's

DEANDRE YEDLIN

Boyhood hero?
My uncle

Best footballing moment?
Playing against Belgium in the World Cup in 2014

Toughest opponent?
Eden Hazard

Team supported as a boy?
Seattle Sounders

Pre-match meal?
Pasta

Any superstitions?
I don't have any

Favourite current player?
Dani Alves

Favourite other sports person?
LeBron James

Favourite stadium other than St James' Park?
CenturyLink Field, Seattle

What would you be if you weren't a footballer?
In the entertainment industry

Where did you go for your 2017 summer holiday?
Los Angeles and Las Vegas

What do you like in particular about the city of Newcastle?
The vibe around the city

Favourite actress?
Tristin Mays

Favourite TV show?
Power

Favourite music artist/last concert seen?
Future (American rapper)

What do you like doing in your spare time?
Watching movies

Best Friend in Football?
All my teammates

Which three people would you invite round for Dinner?
Martin Luther King, LeBron James, Barack Obama

What's the best thing about being a footballer?
Playing the sport you love

Which boots do you wear?
Adidas

What's the best goal you've scored?
My first Newcastle goal at Derby

Favourite Football Show on TV?
Match of the Day

Favourite football commentator/football pundit?
No one in particular

Favourite PS4 or Xbox game?
FIFA

JONJO SHELVEY

Boyhood hero?
Steven Gerrard

Best footballing moment?
Winning the Championship last season

Toughest opponent?
Luka Modrić

Team supported as a boy?
West Ham

Pre-match meal?
Chicken and pasta

Any superstitions?
None

Favourite current player?
Luka Modrić

Favourite other sports person?
Rory McIlroy

Favourite stadium other than St James' Park?
Wembley

What would you be if you weren't a footballer?
A job in the city

Where did you go for your 2017 summer holiday?
Various places including Orlando, Mexico and the Cayman Islands

What do you like in particular about the city of Newcastle?
Everyone loves football

Favourite actor?
Hugh Grant

Favourite TV show?
Power

Favourite music artist/last concert seen?
Drake

What do you like doing in your spare time?
Playing golf

Best Friend in Football?
Jack Colback

Which three people would you invite round for Dinner?
Michael Jackson, Elvis Presley, Eva Mendes

What's the best thing about being a footballer?
Playing the sport you love

Which boots do you wear?
Nike Vapor

What's the best goal you've scored?
Against Aston Villa for Swansea

Favourite Football Show on TV?
Match of the Day

Favourite football commentator/football pundit?
No one in particular

Favourite PS4 or Xbox game?
No time (I have young children!)

CIARAN CLARK

Boyhood hero?
Zinedine Zidane

Best footballing moment?
Signing my first contract

Toughest opponent?
Paul Scholes

Team supported as a boy?
Celtic

Pre-match meal?
Honey and banana on toast

Any superstitions?
None

Favourite current player?
Too many great players to name!

Favourite other sports person?
Conor McGregor

Favourite stadium other than St James' Park?
Old Trafford

What would you be if you weren't a footballer?
I'd love to keep involved in sport one way or the other.

Where did you go for your 2017 summer holiday?
Spain, Portugal and America

What do you like in particular about the city of Newcastle?
Everyone is so friendly

Favourite actor?
Seth Rogen

Favourite TV show?
Game of Thrones

Favourite music artist/last concert seen?
Drake

What do you like doing in your spare time?
Watching box sets

Best Friend in Football?
There are a few

Which three people would you invite round for Dinner?
You can't beat dinner with your family and close friends.

What's the best thing about being a footballer?
Playing the sport you love

Which boots do you wear?
Adidas Copa

What's the best goal you've scored?
Against Bristol Rovers in the FA Cup

Favourite Football Show on TV?
Match of the Day

Favourite football commentator/football pundit?
No one in particular

Favourite PS4 or Xbox game?
Call of Duty

A TO Z OF UNITED

HERE WE HAVE OUR THIRD INSTALLMENT OF OUR POPULAR A-Z OF UNITED FEATURE.

ARGENTINA – Four Argentine players have played in the Premier League for United (Bassedas, Coloccini, Cordone & Gutierrez).

BROWN ALE – United's iconic sponsor in the mid-1990s and a favourite Geordie tipple.

CHARITY SHIELD – Now the Community Shield and last contested by Newcastle in 1996.

DALGLISH – Father Kenny managed the Magpies whilst son Paul played.

EDGE OF THE SEAT – The feeling during the last few minutes of last May's title decider against Barnsley.

FINNEY – Preston legend Tom was a guest player for United in war-time football.

GINOLA – United's French magician from Keegan's Entertainers side.

HEREFORD – No FA Cup Third Round day is complete without mention of our infamous defeat against the Southern League minnows in 1972.

ILEY-DELIGHTED – The headline when Jim Iley hit the promotion clincher in 1965.

JINX – When will United win the FA Cup again?

KEEBLE – Vic is United's only surviving player from the 1950s FA Cup winning teams.

L **LEAZES** – Leazes Park, Leazes Terrace, no, the Leazes End is the most famous of them all.

M **MILBURN** – The pitman turned legendary centre forward, 200 goals for United.

N **NOLAN** – Captain in 2009/10 and in charge of the other black 'n' whites at Meadow Lane.

O **OLYMPIC STADIUM** – United will play there for the first time in 2017/18.

P **PEANUTS** – Sold to fans at every game at St. James' Park from the 1890s and for the next 80 years!

Q **QUAYSIDE** – One of the favourite areas in Newcastle for post-match celebrations.

R **ROKER PARK** – United won 2-1 on their last ever visit to the former home of their North East rivals.

S **SIR LES** – For Ferdinand, an adopted Geordie and much loved terrace hero.

T **TAIT** – Alex was the first United player to hit a derby day hat-trick in 1956.

U **URWIN** – Tom Urwin is the only player in United's history, and there's been over 1100 players, with a surname beginning with the letter U

V **VETCH FIELD** – The venue in Swansea in 1983 where United played their first ever game on a Sunday.

W **WINGERS** – Great names like Bobby Mitchell, Chris Waddle and David Ginola, and now Matt Ritchie.

X **XMAS** – United's last game on 25 December was back in 1957.

Y **YEDLIN** – The American was a key cog in United's 2016/17 promotion winning team.

Z **ZARAGOZA** – United eased past the Spaniards on the away goals rule in the 1968/69 Fairs Cup winning season.

Fairs Cup Glory

The 1968/69 season proved to be one of the most memorable in United's long history. After qualifying for the Inter-Cities Fairs Cup at the end of the 1967/68 Football League campaign, United kicked off their first European adventure in September 1968 against Dutch side Feyenoord at St. James' Park.

Incredibly the Magpies would go on to lift the trophy, the forerunner of the UEFA Cup and Europa League, on a balmy night in Budapest the following May.

Here we take you through all 12 games with one of the players of the time giving his personal view on how they came through each tie.

1968/69 – INTER-CITIES FAIRS CUP

ROUND 1 (1)

Newcastle	4 (3)	(Scott 7, Robson 35, Gibb 44, Davies 70)	46,348
Feyenoord	0 (0)		

ROUND 1 (2)

Feyenoord	2 (1)	(Kindvall 27, Van der Heide 54)	45,000
Newcastle	0 (0)		

(Newcastle win 4 – 2 on aggregate)

CENTRE HALF OLLIE BURTON: "It was a completely new experience for the players, and indeed the fans, to be playing European football but it turned into a thrilling ride for all of us. And to be 3-0 up at half time in our first game against one of the top sides in Europe was unbelievable. We thought we'd 'cracked it' before the second leg started but they played us off the park in Rotterdam and in the end we were lucky to progress.

I kept telling big John (McNamee) during the game that we'd get through and I think that spurred him on to 'defend for his life'. What it did do though was hit home how tough this level of football really was, against top-level foreign opposition, but it stood us in good stead for the challenges that lay ahead."

ROUND 2 (1)

Sporting Lisbon	1 (0)	(Morais 89)	9,000
Newcastle	1 (1)	(Scott 32)	

ROUND 2 (2)

Newcastle	1 (1)	(Robson 10)	53,747
Sporting Lisbon	0 (0)		

(Newcastle win 2 – 1 on aggregate)

SECOND LEG GOAL-SCORER POP ROBSON:

"Sporting were a renowned European force and we did very well to get a draw out there even though we almost won it. There had been thunder and lightning during the day and it made the pitch very heavy. Our defence was superb though and that, coupled with the great team spirit we had, served us well. In the return at St. James' Park, where we played in an unusual all white kit, the adrenaline was flowing and I was lucky enough to score one of the best goals of my career, volleying in big Wyn's header.

"We pushed for a second to kill the game off but couldn't manage it and I remember it being nerve-wracking towards the end as we hung on to our slender advantage. The Fairs Cup nights were proving to be really special occasions with a real buzz of excitement around the whole city."

ROUND 3 (1)

Real Zaragoza	3 (2)	(Santos 5, Bustillo 20, Planas 57)	22,000
Newcastle	2 (2)	(Robson 6, Davies 31)	

ROUND 3 (2)

Newcastle	2 (2)	(Robson 2, Gibb 29)	56,055
Real Zaragoza	1 (1)	(Martin 43)	

(Newcastle win on away goals rule)

LEFT BACK FRANK CLARK:

"The first game, unusually, was on New Year's Day so we'd flown out the day before and landed at an Air Force base near to Zaragoza. Joe (Harvey) let us all have a New Year's Eve drink which I guess was typical of his management style. The first half was crazy with us equalising twice and in the end I think we were lucky to come away with only a one goal deficit – but with two vital away goals.

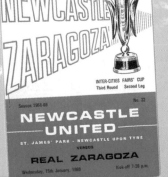

"Back on Tyneside we went into the interval 2-1 up and therefore ahead on away goals and whilst I expected them to really come at us in the second half, we saw the game out comfortably with no real scares. What made it so satisfying was that we were the underdogs and not expected to progress – but we did!"

QUARTER FINAL (1)

Newcastle	5 (2)	(Foggon 23, Robson 36, 75, Davies 65, Gibb 88)	
Vit' Setubal	1 (0)	(Jose Maria 82)	57,662

QUARTER FINAL (2)

Vit' Setubal	3 (1)	(Arcanjo 26, Petita 60, Figueiredo 65)	
Newcastle	1 (1)	(Davies 42)	34,000
(Newcastle win 6 – 4 on aggregate)			

TEENAGER ALAN FOGGON:
"It had been snowing during the day and we weren't sure if the game would be played but the referee gave it the go ahead which was great for us. I don't think many of them had seen snow before and they came out with socks on their hands trying to keep warm!

We got the impression they weren't really up for it and we finished up putting five past them. I got the first, a header, which was a rarity, as most of my headers went flying over the bar! It was completely different when we got across there. Lovely warm conditions and they showed us what a good side they really were.

Who knows what might have happened if we'd played them on a 'level playing field' in each game but that's football. We got through and that's all that mattered."

SEMI FINAL (1)

Rangers	0 (0)	75,580
Newcastle	0 (0)	

SEMI FINAL (2)

Newcastle	2 (0)	(Scott 52, Sinclair 77)	59,303
Rangers	0 (0)		
(Newcastle win 2 – 0 on aggregate)			

GOALKEEPER WILLIE MCFAUL: "It was a great occasion, Rangers were one of the top teams in Europe back then and playing in front of 75,000 at Ibrox was amazing. The nerves were jingling before the game but disappeared once we'd kicked off. It was a very tough game but of course they got the penalty and ironically it was awarded by a good friend of mine, Northern Ireland referee John Adair. I argued with him but on reflection he was probably right! Luckily I saved it so it was back to St. James' Park all square.

"After Jackie (Sinclair) got the second, the Rangers fans came on the pitch and it was horrendous. Ollie Burton shouted 'run' and I did, escaping to the safety of the changing rooms. We finished the game eventually and it was an unbelievable feeling to have reached the final."

FINAL (1)

Newcastle	3 (0)	(Moncur 63, 71, Scott 84)	59,234
Ujpest Dozsa	0 (0)		

FINAL (2)

Ujpest Dozsa	2 (2)	(Bene 30, Gorocs 42)	34,000
Newcastle	3 (0)	(Moncur 48, Arentoft 52, Foggon 68)	

(Newcastle win 6 – 2 on aggregate)

CAPTAIN BOB MONCUR: "It was the biggest game all of us had ever played in but to win 3-0 in the first leg on Tyneside was incredible. The fans were everywhere, watching from roof-tops and hanging out of trees, such was the clamour to see the final. It was goalless after an hour but we'd said to ourselves before the game to be patient and hopefully the goals would come.

"We got battered over there in the first half and many feared the worst but to score so soon after the break totally took the wind out of their sails and it was the icing on the cake to add another two goals to win on the night as well. Joe (Harvey) was really calm at half time, despite the onslaught, and simply told us one goal would do it – and they'd fold like a 'pack of cards'. It was a truly fantastic achievement for this group of players to win the cup."

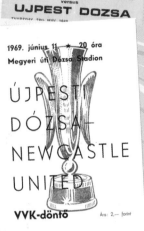

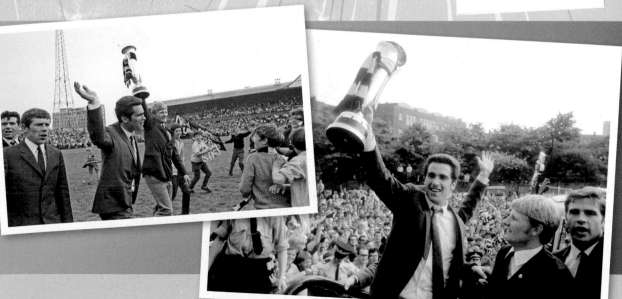

QUIZ ANSWERS

CROSSWORD (PAGE 39)

SPOT THE DIFFERENCE (PAGE 27)

QUIZ ANSWERS (PAGE 21)

Quiz 1
What do you know about United in the past year?

1. Preston
2. Nottingham Forest
3. Dwight Gayle
4. 51,108
5. Ghana
6. Benton
7. Ayoze Pérez
8. Venezuela
9. Liverpool
10. Serbia and Republic of Ireland

Quiz 2
See how much you know about United in years gone by!

1. Argentina
2. 5-1 win v Spurs
3. 6
4. Kevin Nolan
5. 406
6. Solano
7. 2-1 to Newcastle
8. Southampton
9. 2000/01
10. Tino Asprilla

WORDSEARCH (PAGE 47)

Academical
Bale
Beardsley
Bellamy
Exeter

Gayle
Hurst
Lascelles
Leazes
Lineker

Malcolm
Macdonald
Maradona
Milburn
Moncur

Pochettino
Qatar
Southampton
Wednesday
Wembley

SPOT THE BALL (PAGE 23)